ETCHINGS OF THE SOUL

A COLLECTION OF INSPIRATIONAL THOUGHTS

Written By:
Bernadette Garzarelli

Illustrated by: Joan Hennis
Edited by: Nancy Guadagno
            Elizabeth Morrison

Printed by: D & L Litho
            New York, NY

Library of Congress Catalog Card Number: 93-91844
ISBN 0-9639838-0-6

DEDICATION

This book is dedicated to the Source of my inspiration.

The words that follow are reflections of a journey - my journey - that began with an awakening to the world around me and my place in it.

Special thanks to my parents, Stella and Richard and to my sister, Susan and brother, Richard, whose unconditional love is my most cherished gift.

Thanks, also, to my friend and mentor Victor, whose ever-constant encouragement and support kept me afloat when I might otherwise have drowned in writer's frustration.

A COLLECTION OF INSPIRATIONAL THOUGHTS

THE JOURNEY

THE JOURNEY

As you journey through life, remember that how you live today affects all your tomorrows. Remember that turning down the wrong road is part of the journey, and that finding the way back is your challenge. Remember most of all that if you keep God close to your heart, home will never be far away.

There will be expectations not met, promises lost, tears and moments of despair. Remember, however, to be grateful for the sunshine and to find hope in the rainbow. Remember to laugh from your soul and to always hold on to your dreams.

THE JOURNEY

Do not fear the dark side of life, for the journey toward the light is called living.

Look to God to light your path. Look to yourself to walk it.

Do not be discouraged by life's detours. The more turns you take on your journey, the more lessons you will undoubtedly learn.

Spend less time worrying how you are going to live your life and more time living it.

CREATION

CREATION

Imagine a world devoid of sunshine, love, and laughter. Imagine a world without God.

Take delight in man's ingenuity.
Take heart in God's power. One without the other is inconceivable.

When you come to terms with the reality that there are some things man cannot do and some questions man cannot answer, you will come to terms with the existence of God.

You need only hear the wind to know that God is in control.

This life is merely the overture to a much sweeter song.

YOUTH

YOUTH

Look to a child for the gift of laughter, the bliss of innocence, and the treasures of the moment. Look to a child for life.

If we leave our children with but one lesson, let it be one of respect for all life. Without this, all else is worthless.

When seeking truth, listen to the very young for they know no bias.

CONTEMPLATION

CONTEMPLATION

In this busy world, stop and take a moment to pray for the motivation to be the best you can be and the inspiration to know what that is; for the strength to challenge each obstacle you face, and the stillness to enjoy each breath you take.

Beauty has little to do with what we see and everything to do with how we see it.

To ponder God is human.
To intellectualize God, foolish.
To question God, even more foolish.

SEARCHING

SEARCHING

Though you may feel lost in a transition,
remember that for every ending there awaits a
new beginning. Don't hurry; take the time to be
still and to listen.

Listen to what's on your mind . . .
Feel what's in your soul . . .
Follow your heart.

SEARCHING

When seeking answers to questions about life, look to the wisdom of those who lived before you. When seeking answers to questions about your life, look to the wisdom that lives within you.

When looking for that place to call home, look to your heart for that is where it begins and where it ends.

Your dreams become reality the moment you no longer see them as dreams.

Victory is in the drive to succeed.

FORGIVING

FORGIVING

Rise above the pettiness of others; the air is much fresher up there.

Put the energy you might expend on revenge toward accomplishing an act of kindness for another.

You will find that in some of life's uncontrollable situations, the most gentle word one can apply is acceptance.

LONELINESS

LONELINESS

When you feel alone in this great big world, look first to God and then to those He has given you. Put a smile on someone's face. Wipe the tears from a child. Give of your heart, be it broken or whole. For once you have touched the life of another, you will no longer be alone.

In a world where so many are in need, loneliness need never consume you.

FAITH

FAITH

Faith comes from believing that the sun will reappear after every storm.

When you lose someone you love, find strength in your faith. Think not of your loss, but of your loved one's triumph over this world.

JUBILANCE

JUBILANCE

Joy is only as short-lived as your memory allows.

Of all man's senses, it is his sense of humor that will sustain him.

When you have the choice, choose to smile.

Enjoy your days as they are given to you - - one at a time, never forgetting that they are irretrievable gifts.

STANDING STILL

STANDING STILL

It is in the stillness of the moment that we can feel the most serenity, the most courage, and the most alive. It is in the stillness of the moment that we are one with our God.

Why am I in such a hurry? I can't run from the past and am unable to see what's ahead. Teach me, Lord, to stand in the moment, fully alive in its beauty.

SIMPLICITY

SIMPLICITY

In the complexity of technology and science, man has lost the simplicity of what it means to live.

When you become overwhelmed by the trials of this world, stop. Let your feet feel the earth. Shake hands with an Oak. Turn your eyes toward heaven. Let the sound of the surf soothe you, the song of the bird serenade you. Smell the green of the forest, the beauty of a flower. For it is in the simplicity of nature that you will find comfort.

HOPE

HOPE

Look not with fear upon life's mysteries, but
rather with hope in the promise they hold.

If you witness even one kind, generous, loving
act of mankind, you have seen God.

When sadness overcomes you, take some time
to ponder the good things about your life -
successes and friends - then take these
thoughts with you, for they will lighten a heavy
heart.

HOPE

When you reach the point of despair you will understand the value of friendship and the power of God. And thus, amidst your despair you will have cause to rejoice.

Just when we think life couldn't be grander, a cloudburst appears and dampens it a bit. It's that little cloudburst that teaches us humility.

It is in your weakest moment that you will discover your greatest strengths.

HOPE

Isn't it a comfort to know that when the tragedies of this world befall us, God is there waiting to pick up the pieces.

There is no greater suffering than the pain of suffering alone. Share the burden of life's hardships. Trust in God.

FULFILLMENT

FULFILLMENT

Whatever you choose to do with your life, do it with love, gratitude, and humility. Tenderly devote yourself to what you have chosen. Be thankful for the opportunities that await you. Take pride in your achievements, and remember always to remain humble at heart.

Be the best you can be today; nothing more, nothing less. The Lord asks no more of you.

To fully experience the joy of achievement, look not at what you have done, but at the face of the person whose life you have enriched.

FRIENDSHIP

FRIENDSHIP

To truly enjoy humanity, we must overlook our
weaknesses and look instead for the good
heart, the warm smile, the tender touch.

That person who walks through hard times with
you, showing you how to smile along the way; that
person is your friend.

At the moment you give of yourself to help
another, you are in touch with God.

That which seems insurmountable alone can be
quite pleasant when shared.

LOVE

LOVE

Love is the heartbeat of life.

The ability to love is a gift; the courage to love, your challenge.

To love another human being unconditionally is to achieve the greatest of all love.

Man has been given many tools with which to build a life, the ability to learn and the capacity to love the most powerful of them all.

Try hard and you can achieve something. Add love and you will have everything.

MIRACLES

MIRACLES

You need not travel far to witness a miracle.
Watch a flower bloom. Watch a woman give birth.

Life's journey is short, but God's gifts are many.
The brightness of the sun to light your way, the
darkness of the night to give you rest. The
rhythm of the surf to soothe your soul, the
beauty of the countryside to warm your heart. A
child's laughter to lift your spirits, an old man's
wisdom to guide your way. These are the
miracles of life.

Technology will fail us at times. Only the miracles
of nature are steadfast.

One of the miracles of the human spirit is our
ability to smile through our tears.

THANKSGIVING

THANKSGIVING

Take the time to put back into the earth some of its beauty and goodness, for it has served you well. Take time to thank your Creator for breathing life into your being and hope into your spirit, for He has served you well.

They taught us, lectured us, and nurtured us. But probably the greatest gift our elders gave us was their time. Make the time to return the favor.

At the end of each day, thank your Master for the gift of life. Ask compassion for the moments you fell short. Promise to give your best to all those who touch your tomorrow. Then close your eyes and rest. He has heard you.

PEACE

PEACE

The moments we are at peace with ourselves
are the moments we experience heaven.

All that surrounds you is in constant motion.
Look within for stability.

When I reach my final hour in this world, there is
only one success I hope to have achieved, and
that is being at peace with myself and my God.

SELF

SELF

The only conscience you need concern yourself with is yours.

To sacrifice one's self-identity is to self-destruct.

If you are true to yourself, it follows that you will be nothing less than honest with others.

Be firm in your convictions, gentle in your presentation.

There lives inside each of us the fulfillment we seek from others.

Getting in touch with yourself is the beginning of understanding others.

COMPLETION

COMPLETION

As you grow older, surrender the years gracefully and leave behind the cares of youth. Savor the memories that give you pleasure, cherish those who made them possible. Go forth with the wisdom of your years and the tranquility that comes from knowing at last who you are.

"Etchings of the Soul," a collection of inspirational thoughts, was born out of the depths of a heart that was hurting. As experienced by many poets, the creativity that spills from one's soul is often the result of difficult times.

With a deeper faith in myself and a greater understanding of life, I recommend that you not shun life's pitfalls and adversities, but that you embrace them and seek the truth that lies within the experience. As the renowned poet and philosopher, Kahil Gibran, said many years ago: "Your pain is the breaking of the shell that encloses your understanding."

In the words that follow, I share with you my secret to capturing joy and tranquility in a complex, often chaotic and hurtful world. Look for simplicity and silence. Stop a moment to live a lifetime.

A published poet, Bernadette Garzarelli's work has appeared in "Mottos to Live By" and "A Joyful Noise." Additionally, she has authored greeting card verses and human interest articles, and is a freelance writer of print and broadcast advertising. Her second inspirational journal, "Echoes of a Voice Within" is forthcoming. She lives at the Jersey Shore with her best friend and mentor who also happens to be her husband.